Holy Spirit
LED POETRY

Holy Spirit
LED POETRY

Dr. Don Carson

ILLUSTRATED BY: NATALIE MARINO

ARPress
ILLUMINATING IDEAS,
EMPOWERING VOICES

ARPress
45 Dan Road Suite 5
Canton, MA 02021

Hotline: 1(888) 821-0229
Fax: 1(508) 545-7580

Ordering Information:

Quantity sales. Special discounts are available on quantity purchases by corporations, associations, and others. For details, contact the publisher at the address above.

Printed in the United States of America.

| ISBN-13: | Softcover | 979-8-89389-124-9 |
| | eBook | 979-8-89389-125-6 |

Library of Congress Control Number: 2024909776

Table of Contents

Dedication

I want to dedicate this book to my Mom, Phyllis Murray Carson. She raised me in a Christian home and always wanted me to be a minister. She made sure I knew of Christ and because of the influence of my parents I was saved when I was 5. She wrote a book called "Alive in Him" and that is in part what gave me the desire to write this book. I wanted to illustrate the book because this book and I saw how pictures added to the poems. My mom's influence was instrumental in me writing this book. I did not know anything about my mom being a poet until after she died but I think it was instilled in me as a gift from God without me knowing it.

I also want to dedicate this book to my Dad, Luther Carson. He, with my mom helped me grow up in a Christian house and with good godly parents. I had time to learn from him 17 years after my mom passed to see some things about him which I might not have seen otherwise. He was a Godly man who showed his kids the importance of Christ in their life. Since my Dad was involved in the church that made me want to be involved as well. I thank God for both of my parents and because of what I gained from them I am able to have this book published.

Thank You

I want to thank my friend and illustrator Natalie Marino for her time consuming effort in making the illustrations as good as they are. She has always been a friend and patient with me during the writing of this book. Her constant love makes me so glad I am her friend. I have been a friend of hers for many years and am honored to do this book with her.

I want to thank the staff or ARPress especially Miguel Hernandez for his invaluable aid and counsel in helping me to understand the process and with the fellowship that he gave me. I want to thank Bernadette Delvin for her kindness and help as well. I believe that these poems will benefit many, since I believe that they are given to me by God! Thank You Charmaine Hopkins for helping as well!

Most of all I want to thank the Lord Jesus Christ. He paid for my salvation and kept me through many rough times. He kept me when I had nothing and provided for me so I give him praise for the good and bad for he keeps us in all things. I praise Him for what I do have and for what I do not have. I praise Him for who he has put in my life and for how the lives of those people have helped to shape me and keep me. He is worthy of all praise, and without Him not only is this book not possible but I would never be here, so I say He is worthy. So all the work in this book I dedicate to you and give you the praise and honor Lord Jesus that you so richly deserve. I also thank the Lord for bringing my wife and daughter into my life for they have become an important part of my life. Thank you Jesus!

Introduction to the Poetry

Dr. Don Carson has been preaching grace for over 25 years. These poems reflect that teaching. In 2006 Rev Don Carson became the Pastor of Word of Grace Fellowship and at that time he started to write poetry to go with each message. He continues this practice today. The poems in this book are the poems he created for each Sunday sermon and represent the Character of God. They demonstrate the love of God which was given to us in the Gospel of Grace. The poems are divided into 4 areas 1) Who God is 2) What God has for us 3) The basis of our blessing 4) How we can respond to him

These poems were the basis for the messages that Dr. Carson spoke on God's Character and all of these poems were inspired by the Holy Spirit. These poems led Dr. Carson in the direction the message was to take. It is his hope that these poems will inspire you the same way that it inspired his listeners, so that you can also learn in His grace by learning 1) Who God is 2) What God has for you 3) What is the basis of Blessing from God and 4) What is the Basis of our response to God.

Character of God
(53 poems)

This series of poem is based on the concept in the verse 1 Tim 4:14 Neglect not the gift that is in thee. I used this as the verse for the whole series that we should not neglect not what God put in you.

Poems to introduce the series
Neglect not
God's Character

God is... (3 poems each) ages
Amazing Love
Grace
Eternal
Spirit

Has... (3 poems each) face
Faith
Anointed Truth
Compassion and Mercy
Evidence of Peace

Gives (3 poems each) basis
Blessing
Assurance
Salvation
Inheritance (freedom)
Saviors work (Obedience)

My Response (3 poems each) walk
Worship
Active Ministry
Love
Koinonia

NEGLECT NOT

Neglect Not the Revelation of God in You

Neglect not what God has given
To you because of Calvary
Putting all that he has in you
Setting men at liberty

The Father held nothing from men
The Kingdom is now within you
The blood is the down payment
So we know God's Word is true

Jesus Christ is the only way
That we can have eternal life
God sent him down from Heaven
So the church will become his wife

The simplicity of God's grace
Even a child can understand
All that God has provided
Came by Christ who is God's right hand

This revelation now lives in you
God's Spirit shines from your heart
So I can now live in peace
From us God will never part

So let's learn of who God is
And of his Amazing Grace
We'll study God's character
And one day soon we'll see His face

GOD'S CHARACTER

God's Character

God's Character:
God gave all in grace's gospel
Obedience given by his love
Dependent on him as my source
Spirit comforts me from above

Loved forever and a day
Offered Christ and his mercy
Verily I say unto you
Evil ended at Calvary

My Response:
Blessing others in Jesus name
Love walks in saints speaking grace
Eternal fellowship is my aim
Sharing salvation to mankind's race

Sing praises causes of God in Christ
Is why we will worship you
No more sin cause the price is paid
Giving love to man- I know tis' true!

GOD ✝

is amazing love

God's Love in Action

Love shows God's power through others
Some to water; some to plant
Love gives the door to blessing
So I do not think I can't

Don't love people cause of their deeds
Don't focus on their sweet talking
When you do you're no different
Than how the heathen are walking

The love of God will save his people
Keeping us from Satan's lies
Love keeps me holy in his sight
Love is why God hears all my cries

God loved you when he died that day
Christ let them nail him to the tree
He bore the stripes on his back
So that from sickness you'd be free

Love puts others before oneself
Love makes you want to show the way
So all can see who Jesus is
Confess God's work in Him today!

Love's Gift

God so loved the world He gave
His only begotten Son
To die for the sin of the world
So that in Him it might be done

Love removed the obstacles
That kept us from having union
With God our Father, Lord Most High
Now we share with Him communion

Love enabled us to know Christ
So now with God we fellowship
He is a part of all we do
So in Him I have a relationship

Love puts God's gifts in me to work
So I can share with men his grace
He put his power within me
As a sign to the human race

Share his love in signs and wonders
With miracles that I perform
I must stop looking at myself
By His Spirit I will transform

Love's Work

Loves work has never questioned
Why God's love can't see my sin
Since we live in Jesus Christ
In the end one day we'll win

God's love bore all of our wounds
On the cross he bore those stripes
The love of God will never end
So with God I have no gripes

The Law of Moses shows God's love
The prophets of old had said
It is not because I'm so good
Before him my works are dead

I will go to Heaven's shore
I'll live in a mansion one day
I have accepted the holy truth
That Jesus is the only way

Love returns us to the Father
To live in eternal glory
I can't say enough of this gift
At the cross I was made holy

Grace's Gospel

God showed us his great mercy
Giving us the love that we need
HE gave Christ to save our flesh
Sending His word God's righteous seed

God gives without cost to men
By good works we can't justify
I know I don't deserve it
But me Christ did sanctify

He keeps me while in this life
So that we can share His Son
Above everything else I must
Remember Christ said it is done!

Walk in all that Christ has earned
Accept what comes from Calvary
The law is not for you to keep
Since from sin God did set me free

He became God's Holy Lamb
Making us right in God's sight
Our sin died on that holy day
So now we can walk by God's might

Jesus Kept the Law

I couldn't keep that old law
So Christ did pay the ransom price
His is God's own substitute
So now I need to be born twice

The law gives strength to my sin
The law made my sin increase
The law pointed me to God's Son
But at Calvary it did cease

I'm righteous apart from the law
By grace through faith He did keep
No longer is it about me
At the cross my God did weep

No longer must I earn my keep
By doing all that God had said
Way back then if you broke a law
You can end up being dead

Jesus never did any wrong
HE kept all that God did plan
No one else ever came close
Now In Christ I understand

Grace's Obedience

Jesus Christ was made obedient
Even to the death of the cross
HE did nothing to deserve
Death, or to suffer any loss

His obedience is now mine
God cares deeply for your soul
He loved us all so very much
That God just had to make us whole

Instead of the Mosaic Law
God focuses on Jesus Christ
The law was done away that day
It was there that He paid my price

So my goodness is from Christ
Not from keeping those old laws
It was designed to help us see
I need Christ to remove my flaws

So I will now see myself
Through what Christ for me has done
I know now that God is pleased
Cause he made me holy in his Son

GOD IS ETERNAL

Eternal Life

Eternal life is more than just
Having a body that can't die
It is in being together
With my Father the Lord Most High

Eternal life is in knowing Christ
Accepting what He did for me
Living in God's eternal grace
That flows from Mt. Calvary

Eternal life is to be free
Walking in his great love for me
God's spirit moves on me to tell
That Christ gives me liberty

God's love is found in knowing
That your name is in the Lord's book
Christ comes in the clouds of Heaven
Since long ago my sins he took

I will walk on the streets of gold
I'll live in a mansion above
I will eat the food of angels
I will live in my Father's love

Eternal Joy

Eternal joy is in knowing grace
One day I will see God's face
He will make my body brand new
Because of Christ's deeds will I do

Joy is what I have won
By the blood of God's perfect Son
Joy is walking with God today
Kept in the love of Christ my way

Eternal joy is being free
To walk from the fear I see
My sin burned in hell's fire
So I'll lift Jesus name higher

Joy is praising God's holy name
Sharing that from the Father Christ came
Joy is when I share his grace
Telling men how he took my place

Eternal joy is a holy life
Speaking his words remove our strife
Joy is knowing that Christ will return
Since in Hell my sin did burn

I will share this joy with all men
In Christ I am a perfect 10
The work for me is to believe
I'll tell men how they can receive!

Eternity of God

My God is the eternal One
I know him through his worthy Son
God lives in the eternal now
Before Him all men must bow!

There's no end to Heaven or Hell
So of his grace to men I'll tell
Salvation's gift I will not spurn
All that do will forever burn

Grace gave me God's own being
Simply by in Christ believing
Eternal life lives within me
From Eternal death I'm now free!

The light of life shines through me
Cause God's son died at Calvary!
HE gave to man his Righteousness
Through Christ alone and nothing less!

God lives outside of time
His love does ring as a chime
Jesus Christ is Jehovah's Son
The Great I AM said it is done!

GOD IS SPIRIT

Spirit of Grace

Grace is the Gospel's reason
The Spirit reveals God's love
Men still think God condemns them
Not knowing the grace from above

Will you join the winning team?
So you can go through Peter's gate?
The way of God is by the Son
Without Him Hell is my fate

Grace put me in the holy book
That God wrote before time began
Grace keeps me wrapped in his love
And not the works done by man

Grace is not always seen by men
But we feel God's Spirit within
Grace gives to us God's provision
Through His blood I can enter in

Grace is stronger than Adam's sin
To Christ, Satan lost in hell
Grace keeps me in God's holy place
Now this goodness I must tell!

The Spirit of Comfort

I will send another to you
To be your Holy Comforter
His presence will come inside you
Making God your Holy Father

He comes to give you Jesus Christ
All that He both said and did
Ensuring me this benefit
In Him my life is now hid

I am comforted by his grace
Knowing Christ is coming for me
These words give me encouragement
That from death I will be free

He is the God of all comfort
Who gives his kids love and peace
He wants to give me all he has
Because of Christ my sin did cease

The Spirit does not condemn me
Through Christ's blood I'm now free
Since Christ died on that holy day
Now I'll know God's liberty

The Spirit of Truth

The Spirit of truth is come
HE convicts the world of sin
That they need God's righteousness
He'll come cause I ask Him in

The truth of God lasts forever
Peace and life give liberty
Perfection cannot be earned
Since God's gifts come to us freely

The Holy Spirit assures me
That my judgment was long ago
Settled on the old rugged cross
So peace with God is now a go

The law condemns all my deeds
When in Eden Adam did fall
In the garden Christ took my place
So now on his Name I will call

The truth comes from God's holy work
His words tells us the price for grace
The truth is the cost was high
To redeem the whole human race

God's Face

The face of God is Jesus Christ
HE came to Earth as man's savior
To show to us who God is
How can we have holy favor

The face of God is in his faith
Reveals to us Heavens' worth
IT was given to show all men
Christ is the Lord of the Earth

The truth comes by God's Spirit
Who comes by Christ's redemption?
Now he lives within his people
Who are made a new creation!

Compassion shows to us his love
Demonstrating God's great grace and mercy
Only by the work of Christ
Can in life we truly be free

I now have peace with the Lord
Who does not base it on what I do
God says He is everlasting
Trust me for my word is true

Let God's Christ be in you today
Giving to me Jesus holy deed
God will come and live within
So you can have God's holy seed

Faith's Confidence

In the beginning God spoke
Creating all that we can see
HE made it out of nothing
Sharing his love with you and me

What I have from God is within
He put in me all of his deeds
Giving to me his confidence
When he planted in me his seeds

Have no trust in your sinful flesh
There is nothing good within it
When my flesh died on God's cross
In His book my name was writ

When I focus on Christ I win
Adam made me lose this race
So God made Heaven possible
Christ shared with me his amazing grace

For all things I will trust Him
No matter what they might be
He's worthy of all my praise
The Christ of Mt. Calvary!

Dependent on God

Do you depend on your own faith?
Or why your work is enough?
Do you do a pretty good job?
Thinking you can strut your stuff?

Before God my mouth is quiet
There is nothing that I can say
I'm not worthy of his gifts
That His Son is made my way

I live my life by his Son's faith
I need his help for everything
He gave me his grace, faith and love
So of His gifts I will sing

I must not rely on myself
It is not by my morality
That God justifies me by grace
But when Christ's sacrifice I see

I will trust Christ to be my life
He showed me God's holy love
Love is the basis of my faith
All I have comes from God above!

Faith's Power

I love to see the works of God
Happen daily in my life
He does miracles and healing
To preserve the true church God's wife

The power of God flows through me
Signs and wonders show men his love
Demonstrating Christ is risen
And mediates for us above

Jesus Christ is always the same
He will keep His Word to me
Now his Word is in my life
Since Easter morn I've been free

As I believe I use the name
Stand in all my authority
Devils flee when I say Jesus
His victory gives me liberty

Walk without doubt; let go of fear
I Let the Spirit guide me today
Revealing all Jesus has said
And how He came to be me way

Verily I say

Verily I say to you today
That you my friend will be with me
In Paradise with those who died
There from sin I'll set you free

Christ can only tell you the truth
God cannot tell even one lie
Satan was defeated in Hell
Where Jesus made the devil cry

Verily I will tell you God's truth
You cannot earn your salvation
You must receive it as a gift
I, the Lord, paid your redemption

Verily, I tell you to do good
Be just and honest before all
The curse has been removed from men
Now God has given to you a call

Truly you heard about God's grace
The cross did show his love for you
I walk in Christ I walk in truth
The work of faith I will do

I Am Truth

I'm the way, truth and the life
No man comes to the Father
But by me, said Jesus Christ
My Lord God and redeemer

The truth of God is a person
The teaching of Jesus is true
He bought Heaven down to Earth
Now his works I can really do

The truth is about who I am
Who God has made me to be
It is what I am inside
And how God has made me free

The truth of God is eternal
Time won't change what God has said
Christ came with great signs and wonders
So now I know the law is dead

Truly all flesh is as grass
And sin did cause separation
But now the price has been paid
So mankind can have salvation

True Knowledge

True knowledge is to know the Lord
To know God's love and his grace
All men one day will see the Lord
All that lived in the human race

The truth of God will set you free
Indeed it will point to God's Son
Truth finds no fault in your heart
In Christ all the work has been done

Do you see yourself living free?
Or are you bound to the law?
Has the law really died for you?
Or do you still see a flaw?

The Pauline Revelation
Explains the Gospel of God's grace
Telling us how God created saints
Out of the fallen human race

The truth reveals God's mysteries
That only the simple can receive
Truth must be revealed to men
It's given to those who believe

GOD Has Compassion and Mercy

Offering of Sin

The Lamb of God came from Heaven
To be my offering for sin
The High Priest did approve him
Now God says I can come on in

I cannot pay for my sin
The life of God is what it cost
My salvation has great value
To restore to man what is lost

I am worth the life of God's son
God thinks so highly of me
The Creator was crucified
So that from sin I would be free

I no longer will pay for sin
God's payment was more than enough
He overpaid all of sin's debt
So God gave to me all Christ's stuff

Men do not accept their sin died
Instead they try to do their part
The law was completely kept
From God I'll never be apart

Ordained in Peace

Our works are ordained by God's peace
We are kept by God's own righteousness
It is not by my fleshly works
But by Jesus and nothing less!

My righteousness with Jesus
Changes my works in his sight
I've been declared right with God
So He put within me his might

Once you have peace with the Father
Then you can have peace with man
My works do come from the heart
By God's grace I know I can

His peace lives within my heart
God's Spirit is made one with me
In my heart He will not part
For I was blind but now I see

His peace has opened my eyes
Heaven's glory I can now see
Grace is God's source of what I see
The gifts flow down from his Son's tree

Our Compassionate Savior

Your compassions never fail me
Your mercies will hold me up
You love me like no other
Thank God Jesus drank that cup

Sin is now a dead issue
At the cross sin was crucified
Jesus was my substitute
Now I have been justified

The 1st Adam brought death to man
The 2nd Adam gave us life
He nailed the law to that tree
Now God and man have no strife

God's grace has appeared to all men
His compassion has now been shown
God's vision is in Jesus Christ
In his Word I have really grown

One day to Heaven we will go
When we hear the angelic shout
Our bodies will be made new
Never again to wear out

GOD HAS PEACE

Heart of Mercy

Mercy comes from God's big heart
From this gift I will not part
God's grace is the source for me
By his mercy I have liberty

The merciful Holy Ghost
Lives within me so I cannot boast
All that God has given to me
Flows from the blood of Calvary

By mercy I keep God's law
Christ sees me without a flaw
From grace's throne I obtained mercy
His love reveals I am now free

How can I bless you today?
God's mercy shows me the way
I do not deserve this gift
Thank God he removed sin's rift

Let us walk with a merciful heart
Loving men is only a start
His mercy will be shown in me
Proving to men that I am now free!

Acts of Mercy

God showed mercy at Calvary
Giving his love to set all men free
Mercy's deeds come from Jesus' love
And from the God who reigns above

Mercy rejoices over judgment
So Jesus God's Son was sent
To die as sin on Calvary
So in Him I was made free

God's mercy is new every day
Showing God's love is the only way
His mercy endures forever in Christ
Cause he paid sin's horrible price

When I do a merciful deed
It reveals God's love as a seed
Mercy comes from within my soul
So through me God can make men whole

Kindness is a divine gift
So we can give others a lift
Mercy is God acting through me
Sharing peace that comes from God's tree

Receiving Mercy

Mercy is something we all need
God's truth frees me from sin's deed
I must realize I need his aid
By Jesus' blood my sin was paid

Some people can't accept a gift
Even though it gives them a lift
God is worthy to be praised
From Hell itself I was raised

Grace extends mercy to me
So that I can set others free
When I let his mercy flow
Then Christ within me will grow

I can't give until I receive
To see new things I must believe
Mercy reveals truth in my soul
God's life then comes making me whole

What I receive I'll give to you
Showing us both God's word is true
Jesus Christ is God's holy door
One day soon through the clouds I'll soar

I'll walk in his mercy and grace
So I can show man his face
Walk with me in what Jesus gave
So his gifts we both will crave

GOD GIVES BLESSINGS

Basis of Salvation

The blessing of Abraham
Is given to Christ's holy seed
Not because of your DNA
But Provides man all that we need

I now have God's assurance
He comforts me with His love
My life is hid in God's son
And the Spirit which coves from above

Salvation is God's idea
Tell all men for them Christ died
I now share God's great grace
When at Calvary God cried

I'm an heir of God in Christ
I receive freely by his grace
I do not deserve what God gives
Thank God His Son took my place

Calvary's blood was sent to man
From Adam's sin until today
The Savior's work will never end
Jesus alone was made my way

Come to Christ so God can show
How in Him you can be free
Receive his love in you today
Through the God of Calvary

THE BLESSING OF ABRAHAM

Abraham's Blessing

Abraham's Blessing is now mine
The Gentiles have now been grafted in
Jesus is the Divine vine
Which came down so man could come in

I will now share God's blessing
Which God gave to me by Christ
I have the power of his Name
Because for me He paid my price

HE became sin and bore sickness
In Hell my atonement was paid
So I will bless you by God's work
With the foundation that was laid

Heal the sick and raise the dead
Make the lame walk and the blind see
You open the prison doors
Setting all the captives free

Go in the power of Christ
Performing His works today
Walking in His love and mercy
Showing others why Christ is your way

Bless Others

Bless all men in Jesus Christ
That is what we are told to do
I must work while it is still day
So I'll show the Gospel to you

The blessing lies inside of me
Since Jesus Christ died on the tree
HE became my substitute
So Christ is now my Jubilee

Make the lame walk and the blind see
Speak in tongues and raise the dead
Heal the sick through his holy name
That is what the Bible has said

I'll speak the power of his grace
Letting the Spirit be my guide
I'll focus on the price He paid
There is no more room for my pride

He does His work through my hands
Opening the door for God's grace
HE will lead me in what to say
Until I see his holy face

Hear Him

I gave you everything I have
Cause you are so precious to me
You left all of Heaven's glory
To come and set all men free

You crucified my huge debt of sin
By the blood that shed for me
So I will honor you today
Cause of the Christ of Calvary

I will honor you in my life
In my deeds I will show you love
You sent me the Holy Ghost
So you can guide me from above

No matter what happens today
I will give you praise in my life
You brought salvation to all men
Calling the church Christ's own wife

I will praise you God Most High
For all the work you did for me
Eternity won't be enough
To praise the Lord who set me free

GOD GIVES ASSURANCE

Life's Story

I love you not because of deeds
Or not because of what you say
If I do that I am the same
As people who do not know the way

Love should put others before me
Love should focus on what is right
How can I bless this person
Bring them to your holy light

Love allows me to do God's work
To put in you God's holy seed
To minister God's special touch
In your life you'll see God's deed

When I was still God's enemy
Jesus took my stripes on His back
He took God's wrath in my stead
Before God I now have no lack

So I'll love the Lord Jesus Christ
He redeemed me from this earth
Setting me apart from all men
Just because of the 2nd birth

Lord, I will praise your holy name
I will lift your love on high
I will share with all men your walk
Until I meet you in the sky

Comforting Lord

You were there when I am weak
Every day of every week
When I don't walk or even speak
You alone will I only seek

The Comforting Holy Ghost
Tells me my sin God did roast
I have joy instead of sadness
Thru Christ and His righteousness

You remind me of what Christ said
When he was raised from the dead
He is my only salvation
Raised for my justification

You comfort me by being here
Christ's robe of righteousness I wear
You love me deep from within
So I can lead me to come in

Your eternal joy lets me know
How by Christ to others I can show
How to focus on His perfect peace
Calming me down, cause grace won't cease

God Comforts His People

The saints will go marching in
Through the pearly gates of Heaven
I will comfort you with this event
The rapture is truly God sent

Comfort each other by my grace
Share with all in mankind's race
God clothed you in perfection
Since Christ pad for man's redemption

Rejoice in who your Daddy is
That all eternity is his biz
Nothing escapes from his holy sight
By Christ own work you are made right

Tell each other what Christ has done
Share with others life in God's Son
Comfort saints with what I say
Point to Jesus, He's the way

I will assure you in His stead
When the Bible itself is read
Jesus is all that we need
God sowed Him in us as a seed

SAVIOR'S
WORK

Gift of Obedience

I am obedient by a gift
Christ earned it all just for me
It was sealed by his pure blood
Making me right eternally

God gave all mankind the gift
So will you just accept it
To God's Christ I have said yes
Which saved me from the Hell's pit

Men still teach this law must be kept
Ignoring what Jesus has done
I would rather trust in his work
So I can have fun in his Son

The redemption has been paid
It was posted to my account
God looks at the eternal blood
That flows from Calvary's mount

God gave to me this holy gift
Just so that I could enter in
Heaven was made for us to dwell
By God's grace I have no more sin

Obedience is a Gift

Obedience is God's gift
Christ himself removed sin's huge rift
God wrote the commands in stone
Now God's light in me has shone

IN Christ now my sin is dead
Just like those prophets have said
The stone has been rolled away
Keeping the commandment God's way

The law was until Jesus Christ
When He would come to pay sins' price
I can't serve God through dead laws
But God no longer sees my flaws

My life is hid in Christ alone
God's light in me is now shown
The 10 commands were until Christ
Came to pay sin's eternal price

If my law keeping could keep me
Why did Christ die on Calvary?
So I obey the Spirit's voice
Before by work, now it's by choice

Obey the Spirit

I choose to obey God's voice
Long ago man had no choice
The law gave man condemnation
But now God gives salvation

God gave the law for Christ to keep
Man's best efforts just make us keep
He gave me his perfection
When I received his redemption

God calls unbelief an evil heart
Faith in Christ is where it did start
Obedience is just by grace
By faith I can see God's face

By Christ in me I do obey
Grace thru faith is the only way
God worked out my salvation
By Christ my justification

God said my son you did obey
When I made your sin go away
I see my faith within you
Cause' my Gospel is really true

Inside God leads me by his peace
God's wrath really did cease
I'll walk in His Holy Spirit
Cause I'm right in Christ's pure sight

End of Evil

Evil was defeated in hell
When Satan lost to Jesus Christ
Satan thought that he had beat God
But Jesus met atonement's price

At the name of Jesus all will bow
Then kneel to the Father's glory
Everything changed at the cross
When mankind was made holy

Jesus Christ will return to Earth
To remove evil once for all
Christ will reign for a 1,000 years
On his name all men will call

God will always defeat evil
One day there will on Earth be peace
The day after the Antichrist loses
Then time itself will even cease

The Devil knows his time is short
God himself as sealed his fate
Satan will be thrown into the pit
And evil will end on that date

Eternally Free

Cursed from the start of time
When in Eden man did sin
Satan for a time had control
Not in the end for Jesus did win

At the fall God said Christ would win
God's word sealed the Devil's fate
Men knew tone day Christ would come
And kept waiting for that date

Jesus lived a life without sin
Death had no hold on God's son
Christ died for his creation
Where at Calvary it was done

I'm now free forevermore
Satan must bow to Jesus name
God raised Jesus Christ from the dead
To defeat sin- that is why Jesus came

I will live with God one day
And walk on the streets of gold
God prepared a mansion for me
That is what the Bible has told

Eternal Liberty

Those who were bound seek liberty
We were bound to the law of sin
The law brought death into our mind
But against sin flesh cannot win

Only God could give this freedom
Nothing could free us from that law
All mankind was held in bondage
This inborn sin was mankind's flaw

Jesus came down from Heaven's throne
God became man to take our place
He was made sin as God's lamb
So man can see God face to face

I was bound but now I'm free
Sin was burned up in Hell's fire
No more does God see sin in me
'Cause I know the devil is a liar

Walk in the atonement God bought
Know one day you'll be in glory
Your freedom is secure in Him
Thank God he did this just for me

GOD GIVES SALVATION

Sharers of Salvation

The rich man said he kept the law
But Christ said that he still had a flaw
Your deeds cannot help to save you
Too bad, men don't know its' true

Grace + works = nothing
Grace alone = everything
Jesus Christ has done it all
To redeem man from sin's fall

With God all things are possible
But with man it is impossible
Salvation must be believed
Even to those that have received

I'll share this gift I'm given
My sins have all been forgiven
Jesus was made God's only way
Accept Him in your heart today

God gives us mercy and grace
So one day we can see his face
The Bible says my sin is dead
Yet men don't know what God has said

So share this gift of salvation
Telling them Christ gave redemption
HE paid the price for man's sin
So say yes and enter in

Show His Presence

God lives within the human heart
Said we would never be apart
His presence is within me
So I can help all men be free

Long ago God didn't dwell in man
Because of Jesus now he can
I'm now a new creation
Restored in God's Salvation

God's Spirit lives within me
To give me all Christ has for me
God reminds me what Christ has said
And why his Son rose from the dead

The Spirit does God's work thru me
His Presence helps to keep me free
God hid my life in Jesus Christ
For sin his Son did pay my price

Your presence reveals your love
And the Son who came from above
You gave to me your holy grace
One day soon I'll see your face

Speak His Righteousness

I'll speak his righteousness all day
Of how Christ became my way
God Himself became my sin
HE beat Satan so now I win

Righteousness gives me a new mind
Freeing me from sin's awful bind
HE led captives to God above
So I know that God is love

I'm so glad that my sin is dead
I know God's Word truly has said
That God exchanged my sin that day
Now I'm righteous by Christ God's way

Sin died in the fire of hell
Here is the story so I will tell
I won't focus on what I do
Since I know the Gospel is true

I can't live with a sin consciousness
Instead I'll know His righteousness
I have faith in Mt Calvary
There by the cross I was set free

I must speak of what Jesus did
Or from all men it will be hid
HE took the law out of the way
Thank you Lord is all I can say

MY RESPONSE

Our Response

We worship God from the heart
For he removed all my sin
He provided all that I need
So now in Him I will win

Worship makes us all the same
Praise Him for all the gifts he gave
God has exalted us in Christ
Through his cross we can now rave

From every tongue and nation
There will be men in every place
Not because of what they've done
But by the Holy Spirit's grace

I will bow my knee to the Lord
The name of Jesus is above all
No other name can match it
Redeeming man from the fall

My relationship is with Christ
For God the Son has made peace
I'll walk in his salvation
God did say my sin did cease

I want you to join me today
Will you go to Heaven with me?
Christ already paid your ticket
So cause of grace salvation's free

God's Presence

When God created the whole earth
From the dust HE gave man birth
Jesus Christ God's son, Lord of Earth
Came to give man a 2nd birth

You made your abode within me
From Satan's bondage I'm now free
Wherever I go you do walk
Your Word is the focus of my talk

Your temple is the Holy Ghost
In which no man may ever boast
God's holy Son is Jesus Christ
He paid all of sin's awful price

Be one with God Almighty
Then in the flesh you will be free
I find no fault within you
In my spirit you are brand new

May Jesus God's Holy Son
Reveal that the work has been done
The Holy Ghost makes men free
By God's grace shown at Calvary

Singers of Praise

The singers want to praise his Name
A miracle that day for them came
His mercy has given me peace
Thank God from sin I did cease

Lord, I will praise you today
By the nail prints you made the way
Lord you inhabit all our praise
Like those your son did raise

For so much I can praise you
There is much for me that you do
The Gospel gives to me worth
Thank you for sending Christ to Earth

One day I'll see your holy face
Why? Because you showed me grace
I have a mansion in Heaven
Only by faith can I come in

You are worthy of all my praise
By Christ my hopes you did raise
You created all that I do see
Making me new by Calvary

Lift Jesus Higher

I will lift Jesus higher
In my life and heart today
I will go preach God's whole truth
That Christ is the only right way

John the Baptist introduced Christ
Saying that Jesus must increase
Willingly John gave up his life
Knowing that he must decrease

Jesus said to Nicodemus
When he spoke in John chapter 3
If I be lifted up on the Earth
I will draw all men to me

Jesus told the Pharisees
If the children do not shout
Then the stones will have no choice
But to praise me by crying out

On the final day of judgment
All of God's creation will say
Every man, demon and angel
That Jesus Christ is the only way

Living Christ

Jesus died on Calvary
Long ago when HE took sin's price
He put his spirit within me
To show His power by Jesus Christ

Heal the sick and raise the dead
You will do greater works then Me
I took your place, in Me you live
Showing men Christ has made you free!

I minister to Jesus Christ
By what he does inside me
God does miracles today
Pointing men to Calvary

On Pentecost the Spirit came
To the Christians that were there
HE gave to us special armor
And the reasons we must share

The early church did great works
By those who did truly believe
The same God lives inside us
Who by Christ we do receive

Minister His Grace

How can I not minister grace?
When God has given it to me?
I don't get what I deserve
But by the love of Calvary

Paul said when you go to God's throne
Know my child I will set you free
By the grace that was supplied
For sin on Mt Calvary

I must accept God's provision
So I can give to men with love
Righteousness is one of God's gifts
That is given to me from above

Grace must be a revelation
That is inside of your heart
God is the one who puts it there
So from Christ I won't part

I'll give what Christ put within me
So sinners can see God's face
God is holy and righteous
So he says accept my grace

Show His Power

Jesus Christ did mighty works
Then said that we can do the same
He gave us God's Holy Spirit
And the power of his Name

My God does the impossible
So I will accept what He has said
He even let me use Jesus name
Soon many will rise from the dead

You are God's miracle worker
God invested Himself in you
God trust you with his Son's life
Through you He'll show what He can do

I'll release God's miracles
His power daily I will show
I must listen to his Spirit
Then in his power I will follow

Calvary made me righteous
His resurrection made me holy
I'm worthy now by what HE did
His justification made me free!

Walk in His Righteousness

Men focus on their morality
Looking at what their flesh did do
They think you must keep the law
But God says that is not true

Now I was made His Righteousness
When as my sin Christ did die
I must know this in my heart
In hell all my sin did fry

I'll wear the robe of righteousness
Which came to me by Jesus Christ
I live without fear and worry
Knowing that Christ has paid my price

From righteousness God's blessings came
Wrapped up in an empty tomb
Showing people how God sees me
Without any doom or gloom

How confident am I
In the robe that Christ gave to me
I'll wear it proudly before men
To reveal God has made me free!

Benefits of Worship

Worship will set the captives free
It helps to bring Jubilee
So I will share God's blessing
That is why to you I do sing

Will you come and worship with me
So you too can be made free
God will show his power to me
By His Spirit you have liberty

Worship lets me see God anew
Based on what God says is true
I just get lost in God's love
Now I see things from above

David let the worshippers out
Leading the armies with a shout
Praising the God of Israel
Even the Mighty Goliath fell

I will share the Holy Word with you
Telling them the Gospel is true
To help others say I believe
So with worship they can receive

Love God

God's love was shown in Christ
He revealed faith to every man
No longer is it by my works
But by God's Son saying I can

Now that God's love is within me
I will respond to his grace
I can love Him with all that I have
So I'll give it to the human race

I'll love God with my whole heart
Now that I am right in his sight
The law made me focus on deeds
Instead of seeing God's pure light

I'll love you Lord for you loved me
When your Son died on Calvary
I know I did not deserve it
But I'm glad that you live in me

One day I'll see Heaven's glory
And look into your holy face
You made a mansion for me
Cause of your amazing love and grace.

Love Self

I must learn to love myself
I must learn that God loves me
I must learn that I'm in Christ
Cause in Him I'm now free

I must learn that God is for me
Jesus Christ showed me how to love
SO I can walk in what He did
To know the God who lives above

HE gave his life for me one day
I will let God live inside me
Selfishness in me must not live
It died on Calvary's tree

Loving me is letting God through
I'm made righteous through his grace
Worthy of God's love each day
No one's flesh will see God's face

Once I learn that God loves me
Then I can live righteously
I must become happy inside
By letting God's love set me free

Love Others

Jesus said that because He lives in you
You will love all men with your heart
It is not in keeping the rules
Knowing that from God we don't part

We love men by our morality
Trying to live right every day
The focus should not be on my deeds
But that Jesus was made my way

Loving others comes from my heart
God is now made a part of me
I must learn that God comes first
Only then will I be really free

Kisses and hugs demonstrate love
Love is also in what you do
Being made meek and humble
Is letting God flow through you

Love is letting God in your life
Love flows to men when you pray
Love flows from inside God's heart
Love gives life in what you say

KOINONIA

Koinonia

Koinonia is a love fellowship
With God I have a relationship
God and I share one body
By faith in Mt Calvary

You inhabit the body of Christ
God did meet the cost of sin's price
Jesus bought the church by his blood
Paid in full by Calvary's flood

In my fleshly body I live
God to me will always give
Man is God's special creation
Saints are a brand new re- creation

Love puts others before you
Love comes from one who is true
I have faith in both God and you
So I'll trust what you say and do

Open your heart to God today
Love man showing He is the way
Minister love to everyone
Telling others God's work has been done!

Fellowship in The Spirit

I want to spend time with you
Lord, your word is holy and true
My flesh may not be worthy
But in you I've been made holy

Sin separated man of old
That is what the Bible has told
In Jesus my sin has died
Thank God the blood has been applied

Alive to God but dead to sin
God in Christ caused me to win
I'll spend time with God Most High
So God's love I will apply

I fellowship without judgment
God's grace to me has been sent
God's strength comes by holy joy
God's love is shown by Mary's boy

Jesus said you are my friend
Know your sin came to an end
Before God I will ever be true
Thank you Lord for all you do

Fellowship with Peace

Words have in them death and life
Problems In life will cause strife
Trust the people God does give
In Christ's love I must daily live

I must live with men in peace
Their problems in my life will cease
Peace and love need each other
In Christ you are my brother

Gossip hinders the flow of love
You are God's light from above
In my flesh I cannot boast
But God made my sin into toast

I will walk with peace in my heart
My friends and I will never part
Let's walk in God's amazing grace
His glory flows from your face

We have a big decision today
Christ makes it so that we don't pay
So today Lord to you I pray
Let me show love in what I say

www.ingramcontent.com/pod-product-compliance
Lightning Source LLC
Chambersburg PA
CBHW051546120626
46551CB00013B/1390